Jack Cornwell

BOY 1ST CLASS, JOHN TRAVERS CORNWELL, V.C., OF H.M.S. "CHESTER."

The Battle of Jutland, May 31—June 1, 1916.

By F. O. Salisbury, painted for the Admiralty on board H.M.S. "Chester." From the print published by the Fine Arts Publishing Co. Ltd. on behalf of the Jack Cornwell Memorial Fund.

"Mortally wounded early in the action, he nevertheless remained standing alone at a most exposed post, quietly awaiting orders, till the end of the action, with the gun's crew dead and wounded all round him. His age was under 16½ years."—*Admiral Sir David Beatty's Despatch.*

Jack Cornwell

The Story of John Travers Cornwell, V.C. "Boy—1st Class"

By the Author of
"Where's Master?"
"Like English Gentlemen," etc.

"I feel that this boy, who died at the post of duty, sends this message, through me as First Lord of the Admiralty for the moment, to the people of the Empire,—

'Obey your orders: cling to your post:
Don't grumble: *Stick it out!*'"

Sir Edward Carson.

The Naval & Military Press Ltd

Published by
The Naval & Military Press Ltd
Unit 10 Ridgewood Industrial Park,
Uckfield, East Sussex,
TN22 5QE England
Tel: +44 (0) 1825 749494
Fax: +44 (0) 1825 765701
www.naval-military-press.com
www.military-genealogy.com
www.militarymaproom.com

In reprinting in facsimile from the original, any imperfections are inevitably reproduced and the quality may fall short of modern type and cartographic standards.

Printed and bound in Great Britain by CPI Antony Rowe, Chippenham and Eastbourne

TO

THE GLORIOUS MEMORY
OF UNKNOWN HEROES

CONTENTS

CHAPTER I
PAGE
"BOY—2ND CLASS" 11

CHAPTER II
IN TRAINING 23

CHAPTER III
THE BATTLE OF JUTLAND . . 43

CHAPTER IV
"FAITHFUL UNTO DEATH" . . 65

CHAPTER V
THE UNKNOWN HERO . . . 75

"BOY—2ND CLASS"

CHAPTER I

"BOY—2ND CLASS"

IF you had been standing on the platform of a certain London station on the 14th of October, 1915, you might have noticed a group of a dozen or so boys. The eldest was about eighteen, the youngest was just under sixteen, and his name was John Travers Cornwell. Although he and his companions were still dressed in ordinary clothes— their Sunday-best, I fancy—they were actually on that day all members of His Majesty's Navy.

Only a little time before these

JACK CORNWELL

boys had been at school, or selling newspapers in the streets, calling out the latest news of the war, or acting as messengers—in some way or another trying to do the work of men who had gone to fight the Battle of Liberty. But now they were " Boys—2nd Class," entitled to draw pay at the rate of sixpence a week and " all found," which means that they were to be fed and clothed at the cost of the country.

And the country was very glad and proud to do this for them, for it needed these boys for His Majesty's ships, the ships which have guarded, and will ever guard, this glorious land of ours from every foe. The Navy had called for boys—but only for boys of the very best character, whose record was altogether clear and clean. His Majesty's Navy will have no others, for the work it does, and the work its boys do, is so tremendously important that it can only be done by those who are, at all times, to be trusted—absolutely. By the time a boy reaches Jack Cornwell's age—and before that—it is known whether he can be trusted—or not. This little book is written to tell the story of a boy whom the Country trusted, and of the way in which he repaid that Trust.

Jack Cornwell, as he was always

JACK CORNWELL

called, was the second son in a happy little family of three boys and a girl. His father and mother were both country folk, one coming from Cambridge, the other from Bedfordshire. There had never been much money to spend in their home in a small street at Manor Park, and it had not been easy to make both ends meet since war broke out, for the father, who was a retired soldier, and long past military age, had joined the Army again when he heard Lord Kitchener's call for more men. Although Jack Cornwell had few of what people call advantages—he left school when he was fourteen—he had a patriot for a father. And that's a very big advantage indeed.

JACK CORNWELL

His mother, too, was always full of cheerful courage. She set to work to keep things going while her husband was at the war, and was helped by her eldest son, who worked at a factory, and by Jack himself, who had secured a job, after he left school, as a delivery boy on one of Brooke Bond's tea vans.

Jack had always wanted to be a sailor. Longingly he had watched the vessels on the Thames, ever sailing forth to the ends of the world, ever steaming into dock laden with treasure from far-distant lands. As a schoolboy he had listened so eagerly to the tales told by "old boys" who returned to visit their classmates when on leave from the Navy. His school had sent many boys to His Majesty's ships and there were at one time at least a dozen on board the "Impregnable" alone.

There came a day when Jack Cornwell made up his mind to "join up." "Your country needs you," he read on a hundred posters. Needed him?—Well, he was ready and willing, glad to answer the call. He went to the recruiting office and asked if he could serve in the Navy. Yes—*if*? Jack Cornwell had brought with him letters from the head of his school and from his employer. His character was "very good." Yes, his country needed *him*.

Photo. Topical Press.

JACK CORNWELL.

"Just an ordinary boy."

JACK CORNWELL

Jack Cornwell was just an ordinary boy. No one spoke of him as especially clever or ambitious. He was quiet and reserved, slow of speech as of anger, seldom gave any trouble, was always straight and truthful. One of his teachers summed him up as a schoolboy by saying, "We always felt we could depend upon him." And that is the stuff that heroes are made of.

In the school that Jack attended the boys are put on their honour; they are taught that straightness, truthfulness, a good character, are the things that are worth while in life, that to do the work before them, whether the teacher is present or not, is the thing that counts.

JACK CORNWELL

Each boy feels that the reputation of the whole class is in his hands, that he cannot do as he pleases, because, if he does, others suffer besides himself, that just as a regiment of soldiers depends for its name and fame on the pluck and bravery and endurance of every single man in it, so the success or failure of a school or a class depends on the honour and sense of duty of every single boy.

Duty and Honour—those were the watchwords of Jack Cornwell's schooldays. You shall read how well he remembered them afterwards, how he lived and how he died with the clear call of those words ever in his ears. Just a boy, just a very ordinary boy, but without thought of self he answered that call—when it came ringing to him out of the roar of battle. Duty called, Honour called. His answer cost him his life ; it gained for him everlasting glory.

Just an ordinary boy, but because he obeyed that call of Duty and Honour—think of it ! his name goes down to the ages with the names of those grand old heroes Drake, Frobisher, Blake and Nelson. Think of it !—when, in the years to come, people read of the great war, the story of Jack Cornwell will be part of the history of the British Empire.

IN TRAINING

CHAPTER II

IN TRAINING

NOW let's see just what a "Boy—2nd class" learns and does when he joins His Majesty's Navy.

Jack Cornwell was trained at Keyham Naval Barracks near Plymouth Sound. There were about six hundred boys in this Royal Training Establishment, which was different from other naval schools in one rather startling way. It was entirely on land. At first you may well smile at the idea of teaching a young sailor his business on land instead of on the sea, but, in the early stages at any rate, it has many advantages. For one thing—and you may certainly smile at this—it is not easy to teach a boy anything at all when he is seasick ; for another, there is much more space in which to keep the models and all the hundred and one things that are used in the daily classes, and you can learn all about the lead and compass and the theory of seamanship and gunnery just as well in a classroom as you can on a ship. The practical part, which must of course be learned at sea, comes later.

The boys at Keyham were divided into " messes," or classes, of twenty. These messes always kept together and each mess passed through the course of training as a whole. In this way it differed from a school, where certain boys at the end of the term go up to another class and others remain where they are. The course of training meant hard work, "jolly hard work," for the boys then had to learn in six months what in peace time they would have been given two years or so to tackle. It was quick work, it was tough work, but the enemy wouldn't wait, the war wouldn't wait. The boys were wanted.

Here's the order of Jack Cornwell's day. The morning bugle sounds at a quarter to six—half-past five in summer. Rolling up hammocks, prayers, clearing and tidying up the quarters till eight o'clock, then a hearty breakfast.

JACK CORNWELL

Inspection by the officer of the day at half-past eight, and by nine o'clock the classes are in full swing. Dinner at mid-day and then work again till three, except on Wednesdays and Saturdays, which are half-holidays, and, after that, games or practice in rowing and sailing. Tea at five, then "go as you please" till hammocks are slung at half-past eight. By nine o'clock when the bugle calls "Lights out," most of the boys are asleep. It has been a very full day, but they have enjoyed every minute of it. There is plenty of fun as well as work and exercise, and the food is just as good and plentiful as it can be.

What did these boys really learn

JACK CORNWELL

at Keyham? First of all, of course, Seamanship. It's a big word and means a tremendous lot, and is divided into many subjects, to each of which a week is given. Jack Cornwell's first week was taken up in learning all about his kit, how to roll his hammock, look after and wash his clothes. Next came a week of semaphore or signalling work, then a week learning "bends and hitches" or what you and I would call knots—it's very important to know how to knot a great rope so that it won't slip—and after that all the mysteries of the compass by which a sailor steers his ship. Jack Cornwell himself had, of course, to learn to steer at the wheel—

there were full-size models worked by electricity at the training establishment—to rig and sail a boat, to throw the lead, by which soundings are taken to find the depth of water. He had to know all about anchors, how to cast them and to weigh them, and he spent a good deal of time on "lights" which mean so much in guiding the sailor through the darkness of the night.

His play was almost part of his work, for he spent many of his spare hours in the boats learning to "row a good oar," and had the joy of belonging to a winning crew in a boat race. He was keen, too, on football and played well. Now and again he and his friends took

JACK CORNWELL

part in concerts at the barracks, and sometimes, when a ship came into dock, they would be taken all over it so that they might see what their future quarters would be like, and how, in actual fact, things on board ship fitted in to all they had learned from the models at their classes. And in the evening they would listen to the yarns their instructors, "old sea dogs," would tell as they sat round the stove in their mess room—yarns of daring and adventure, of storms and fights, of heroism and duty well and truly done.

Jack Cornwell worked with a will at Keyham. Against his name is no record of what they call "crime" in the Navy, no bad marks, you might say. "He was quick and intelligent, he tried hard and behaved well. Yes, a good boy!" so one of his instructors speaks of him. He was always cheery, and that made him popular among the other boys; always spick and span, taking pride in his appearance, and that gained for him the post of messenger to the Commander of the school.

Jack Cornwell was confirmed while at Keyham, and though, like most boys, he spoke little of his feelings, I know that in his quiet way the service meant a great deal to him. He acted upon his faith rather than talked about it—and that's the very best thing a boy can do.

JACK CORNWELL

After three months Cornwell and his mess started their gunnery course. He was taught by a first-class petty officer who was an old Navy man, and at one time a London police sergeant. Now gunnery calls, as you may imagine, for the utmost quickness of eye and hand: everything has to be done at lightning speed. A wrong movement, a slow movement, the slightest mistake in following an order, the least hesitation in carrying it out, and—well, the chance is lost, the whole plan behind the order tumbles to pieces. Although the modern naval gun is a marvel of machinery, it is useless unless it is served by men and boys of quickest brain and deftest hands.

JACK CORNWELL

It is so wonderfully made that it takes wonderful skill to work it, for, as you know, the more complicated a piece of machinery is the more careful you have to be in handling it and the more likely it is to " go wrong."

Now there's great danger that you and I should look upon heroes like Jack Cornwell as so gifted, so naturally clever and brave, so out of the ordinary, that we say to ourselves it is no good our trying to follow in their footsteps because we are not " made that way "— we haven't " got it in us." I am not going to pretend that we all have Jack Cornwell's chance of showing what we can do and endure when the guns are

JACK CORNWELL

booming and the dead and dying lie around us, but I do say, and say again, that this was a very ordinary boy as far as any one could judge at school, at the training establishment, and on his ship. You would think that every one at Keyham would have marked him out as the one boy among all the others. But no—in some ways he was a long way behind his companions. Jack Cornwell found his gunnery course, for instance, full of difficulties. He had learned "seamanship" easily and rapidly; gunnery was very hard, and he was not as quick as he might have been, as others were. He made up his mind he'd do his best to learn, and his instructor

JACK CORNWELL

says he was "quite good" by the end of his course. But no one at Keyham ever spoke of him as brilliant or in any way uncommon. I'll tell you how they did speak of him there, and then you'll understand. "He was a thoroughly decent lad—he had a lot of character—he was a good boy." That's all.

Over and above all this naval training there was something else that Jack Cornwell learnt, about which it is not easy to write, for it is very difficult to put it into words. He learnt discipline. He learnt it in a hundred ways—in the football field, at the mess, in the classes, in the boats, by the fire in the evening ; all day long he was taught that to obey without questioning, without hesitation, is the secret behind all the might and majesty of the British Navy. He began to understand that orders, rules, regulations, are not made by those in authority just for the fun of making them and in order to vex and annoy those under them, but because long years of experience have proved that by obeying these orders, rules, and regulations, and in that way only, can a ship and a ship's company do the work it has on hand. He began to see that those above him, right to the top of the tree, were subject to the same discipline, though it might take

JACK CORNWELL

different forms, that he was an important member of a glorious team, important because *every* player had to do his very best if the team was going to win. Slowly, surely he realised that while he might do everything possible to score for himself, while he had every right to think for himself and to be himself, it was much more important that his side scored, and that often he must sacrifice his own wishes and his own ambitions for the good of the team. Through discipline, Duty and Honour, the watchwords of Jack Cornwell's schooldays, were brought into touch with every-day work.

When the sergeant shouts: "Left! Right! Left! Right!

JACK CORNWELL

Halt! 'Bout turrrn! Forrrm fours!" and you march and turn and do this and that at the words of command you may be tempted to think it is all very silly and useless, to ask what good such drill can possibly do. But watch a boy at his first drill and look at him again after a few weeks' training. At first he hesitates as he hears each order. He has to pause and think before he is certain which is left and which is right; he "'bout turns" the wrong way; he gets into a muddle when he tries to "form fours." But gradually he learns to answer each order correctly, smartly, almost before the word is out of the sergeant's mouth. He hasn't to wait and think, to wonder which way he has to turn; to do the right thing at the right time has become part of his nature. That is the result of discipline. And so in the din of battle, when he can see nothing for the smoke, when his body and brain are numb from the shock of the falling shells, if he hears an order he carries it out in spite of all his weakness, and in spite of hardly understanding what it means—just because drill has trained him to obey. That is what discipline does, and that is how battles are won.

There come moments in all our lives when we have no time, perhaps have no power, to think of right and wrong, of what we

JACK CORNWELL

ought to do. Most of us want so badly to do the plucky, the brave thing, the right thing, when we have the chance, but shall we?— if that chance comes suddenly, without warning, and passes in a flash before we have time to work things out in our minds? Yes,—if we have been so trained, and have so trained ourselves, by discipline that at the very whisper of the call of Duty and Honour we instantly respond as to a command. No,—if we are always thinking about ourselves and what we are going to get out of life and forget that it is what we give and not what we get, what we do and not what reward we receive—that is what matters.

JACK CORNWELL

How did Jack Cornwell learn all this? Largely, I think, from the petty officers who taught him, men who had seen much of life in all parts of the world, men of many years' service, whose pride in the Navy was catching, who, by their example and their teaching and their stories, showed how reasonable and wise and necessary was this spirit of discipline. Discipline was a great part of their lives because it was a great part of the Navy's life, and they lived for the glory of the Navy. And so the splendour of discipline, which so many people think is a dark, cruel, ugly thing, lightened and brightened Jack Cornwell's days. And in that light he died—and lives for ever.

THE BATTLE OF JUTLAND

CHAPTER III

THE BATTLE OF JUTLAND

JACK CORNWELL finished his course at Keyham in April 1916, leaving as a "Boy—1st class" with double his previous rate of pay. He spent a few days at home with his mother, telling her of all his doings and of his hopes that before long he would "get into action and see the Germans beaten." He was ordered to join his ship, His Majesty's Cruiser "Chester," on Easter Monday. It seemed hard that he should have to leave on such a holiday, but when some one pitied him, he laughed and said, "It's just a matter of duty, you see. I should feel ashamed for ever if I got back late and had bad marks against my name."

There are some dates every one of us knows—William the Conqueror 1066, William Rufus 1087, Battle of Trafalgar 1805, Battle of Waterloo 1815, and so on. There's another which we shall never forget—the 31st of May 1916—the date of the Battle of Jutland, the first great naval action fought by the British Fleet for more than a hundred years.

In other books you will read of

JACK CORNWELL

all that the sailors did in the great war, and the full story of this tremendous fight when, after long months of waiting, the German fleet at last came out to give battle and was driven back to its safe harbour, broken and beaten by the glorious British Navy. I am going to write only of the part played in the Battle of Jutland by His Majesty's cruiser " Chester," upon which Jack Cornwell had then served for just over a month.

Time and again since the war began the British Grand Fleet under Admiral Sir John Jellicoe has swept the North Sea in search of the German fleet, and on May 30, 1916, it once more left its base in the far north of Scotland. The battle cruiser fleet, with Vice-Admiral Sir David Beatty in command, was further south scouting for the bigger vessels. On May 31, the German fleet under the command of Admiral von Scheer had also put to sea, and steamed northwards with a large force of battle cruisers and light cruisers and destroyers in advance as a screen in front of the battle fleet. Great was the joy on board the British battle cruisers when at half-past two on that memorable day news came that the enemy was in sight. Full steam ahead was ordered, and the ships dashed through the water to try and cut off the German cruisers, who, when they discovered the British were there in force, turned back to join their Battle Fleet. At a quarter to four both sides opened fire. At the beginning of the battle fortune favoured the Germans, who fought well and bravely. In less than half an hour two of our finest ships had been hit and sunk, but in spite of these losses Sir David Beatty still pursued and pounded the German cruisers until, at five o'clock, the whole German battle fleet arrived on the scene. Now the British Admiral changed his tactics. He determined to draw the German fleet northwards towards the British Grand Fleet, which he knew was coming up behind him as fast as it could steam, so he turned north again with the Germans in hot pursuit.

In advance of Sir John Jellicoe's giant ships, now heaving through the waves to meet Sir David Beatty's cruisers, was the third battle cruiser squadron under Rear-Admiral Hood—they are names to remember, these—and he was ordered to join Sir David Beatty with all speed and help to hold the enemy till the heavy battleships could get into action. The "Chester" belonged to this third squadron. At half-past five Admiral Hood saw flashes of gunfire and heard the sound of guns in the distance. He sent "Chester" forward to find out

JACK CORNWELL AT THE BATTLE OF JUTLAND
MAY 31, 1916.

From the painting by F. Matania. By special permission of "The Sphere."

JACK CORNWELL

what was happening and report to him.

His Majesty's ship " Chester " is a fast light cruiser. She had not been built very long, and the Battle of Jutland was her first fight. When the order came from Admiral Hood, every officer, every man, every boy on board the " Chester " knew that at last their great hour had come, the hour for which they had worked and trained so hard. It was just after half-past five, and although at that time the light was fairly good, mist was rising in the distance and out of that haze the German fleet was coming towards them. That mist meant very much in the Battle of Jutland, for you will understand at once that while it is easy to shoot from the edge of the mist at a ship outlined by the sun in the western sky, it is very difficult to hit a target when firing from the light into the distant haze as the "Chester" would have to do.

On board the "Chester" there was that tense silence which always comes before the storm of action. The decks had been cleared, all the officers, men and boys were at their posts, just as they had been hundreds of times before when they had practised—but this day it was the real thing, and no make-believe. Everything, everybody was—Ready.

At the left-hand side of the

shield of the forward six-inch gun, almost touching it, stood Jack Cornwell — ready. Fixed right across his head and over his ears was what is called a telepad. You may have seen people wearing them in telephone exchanges— instead of putting one receiver to your ear this double receiver is clamped over each ear so that you can have both hands free. A wire went from the telepad straight to the gunnery officer of the "Chester," and through that wire would come the most important of all messages for the gun crew, the officer's orders as to when and how to fire. Now you can see why such pains are given to the training of boys like Jack

JACK CORNWELL

Cornwell, now you can see where discipline comes in. You hadn't realised, few of us indeed yet realise, that a small boy of his age can and does play such a big part in the great game of life and death on board a ship in action.

Jack Cornwell was sight-setter to this forward gun on the "Chester." Whether that gun would hit or miss the enemy depended largely upon his coolness and quickness in carrying out the telephoned orders he received. In front of him was a brass disc, pinned through the centre and moving like a wheel. A touch, a turn, of this disc, and the muzzle of the gun was raised or lowered—that is why Jack Cornwell's hands had to be free, and why the telepad was across his head. For *he* had to turn that disc. The gunnery officer in the centre of the ship orders, let us say, to set the gun for hitting at 10,000 yards. The disc is turned until the notch on its edge marked " 10,000 " is straight with the arrow on the brass plate below it. " Up 300 ! " comes the command, and before you can say it, or even think what it means, the disc is turned until the arrow points to 10,300 yards. " Down 400 ! "—another twist and it points to 9,900 yards. It doesn't sound very difficult, does it ? It isn't—if you are so trained and ready that every order is carried out without a single second's wait.

JACK CORNWELL

But you have to be very quick, very accurate, very attentive and obedient to the voice at the other end of the wire. Suppose you were to say to yourself "What? *Up* three hundred? He really means *down* three hundred, I expect. We have been lowering the gun every time lately. I'll put it *down* three hundred instead." And then the order comes to fire. A miss! And your fault, too, for the gunnery officer can see and you can't, and the enemy was steering away and your shot fell short. Your fault! And perhaps that was the last chance of hitting, and perhaps as a result of that wrong move your ship is hit instead, and very precious lives are lost and a grand ship sunk. It may mean the loss of the battle itself, and the loss of that battle may even mean the loss of the war. Who can tell ?

It is not so very difficult in practice if you are willing to forget all about yourself and give your whole heart and soul and body to the work of carrying out each order as it comes through—but it's not so easy when the real thing comes.

The " Chester " was in action for about twenty minutes. What minutes they were ! A quarter of an hour after she left the third battle squadron she was in the thick of the fight with three or four enemy cruisers. It was at least three to one, you see, but the "Chester" never wavered. She fought all three, beat them off, and twenty minutes later—at about five minutes past six that evening—she rejoined the battle cruiser squadron, her work nobly and successfully done.

I wish I could picture for you those twenty minutes. But no one can. Even those who fought through them and lived to tell the tale cannot do it. The noise, the shock, the strain are so tremendous that the memory of the fight is dimmed and all confused. Every man is so intent upon what he himself has to do that he has neither time nor wish to think of, or to see, what is happening to any one else or even to the ship herself. There are no spectators, no onlookers on board a ship in action, no one to keep the score, no umpire, no reporter. From Captain Lawson on the bridge to the stoker by the furnaces down below, to Jack Cornwell standing by his gun, every one on board had his tremendous duty to perform, and when after that twenty minutes the "Chester" returned to the squadron, still in fighting trim, it was because they all had forgotten themselves and thought only of that duty.

The forward gun turret of the "Chester" received, the minute the battle began, the full force of the enemy's fire. What that force is none who have not been through such a fight can even imagine. Tons of metal flying through the air at the rate of 3,000 feet a second explode upon the deck, thud upon the armour that protects the gun. The noise almost splits the ears, the flashes blind the eyes, and the smell of burnt cordite and of burning paint choke the breath.

Jack Cornwell stands by his gun, his hand on the disc. There is a crash that almost flings him off his feet. A man falls at his side, cut in pieces by the splinters of an enemy shell—dead; another flings up his arms and tumbles,

JACK CORNWELL

horribly maimed, across the deck, then another, then another. A fragment of shell rips across his body, piercing, stabbing, tearing his flesh. The gun's crew, the crew of *his* gun, are being killed one by one, two by two. In a few minutes there are only three left of the nine who stood by him as they went into action. Then a shell bursts right over the gun and—two only are left and they are under cover. Jack Cornwell is standing all alone, with nothing to shelter him against the shot and shell, and he has been terribly wounded. Alone. Around him the dead and dying; himself torn, bleeding, very faint from pain and the horror of the sights and sounds of battle. For war is very, very horrible.

Jack Cornwell's job was done. There was no one left to fire the gun. No orders were coming through the wire to him; there was no one to carry them out if they had come. He could lie down with the others—it would ease the pain a little, perhaps. He could creep away below deck where the wounded were being looked after—there were doctors there who would help him and give him something to stop the pain. He had done his job. No one could blame him if he thought of himself now.

Then there came to his mind, from the memory of his Keyham days, the old Navy order that a gun

JACK CORNWELL

must be kept firing so long as there is one man left who is able to crawl. No! no! no! his job was not done. He might still be needed. There might still be work for him to do. His duty was to stand by the gun and wait for any orders that might come through, stand until he was relieved, stand in the hope that others might take the place of those who had fallen, to *stand* by his gun until he dropped. And he *wouldn't* drop. He clenched his teeth, clenched his hands, almost forgot the pain as he strained to hear if a voice called at the other end of the wire, his hand still stretched out towards the disc to carry out the order if it came. All alone—listening, watching, Jack

JACK CORNWELL

Cornwell stood by his gun—"awaiting orders." And so he stood until the fight was over and the "Chester" steamed back to the fleet battered, bruised and splintered, but still ready for another fight.

"FAITHFUL UNTO DEATH"

CHAPTER IV

"FAITHFUL UNTO DEATH"

"CHESTER" had played her part well. She returned with what was left of her crew and her guns to the third battle cruiser squadron, which at once came into action. Our losses were heavy; splendid ships and splendid men had been sunk, for let us never forget that, as Admiral Jellicoe himself said, the Germans fought gallantly. But they already knew they were beaten, for their losses were heavier still, and when, later, the British Battle Fleet joined in the fight, the remnants of the

JACK CORNWELL

German High Seas Fleet turned and fled to port under cover of the night. The Battle of Jutland was indeed a glorious victory.

When the fight was over and the wounded were carried below, the doctors saw that there was little hope for Jack Cornwell. As soon as it was possible, he was taken ashore and placed in a hospital at Grimsby. He could still talk a little, and though in great pain and nearly too weak to speak, his quiet cheerfulness never left him. The matron asked him how the battle had gone, and he replied in simple sailor-like fashion, *"Oh— we carried on all right!"* These were almost his last words. His

JACK CORNWELL

mother had received a telegram from the Admiralty and was on her way to her boy. At the end, just before he died, he said, "Give mother my love. I know she is coming."

And now I want you to read what the captain of the "Chester" wrote to the boy's mother, because it tells, in words which are already a part of British history, the story of Jack Cornwell's heroism:

"I know you would wish to hear of the splendid fortitude and courage shown by your son during the action of May 31. His devotion to duty was an example for all of us. The wounds which resulted in his death within a short

JACK CORNWELL

time were received in the first few minutes of the action. He remained steady at his most exposed post at the gun, waiting for orders. His gun would not bear on the enemy: all but two of the ten crew were killed or wounded, and he was the only one who was in such an exposed position. But he felt he might be needed, and, indeed, he might have been; so he stayed there, standing and waiting, under heavy fire, with just his own brave heart and God's help to support him.

"I cannot express to you my admiration of the son you have lost from this world. No other comfort would I attempt to give to the mother of so brave a lad, but to assure her of what he was and what he did, and what an example he gave.

"I hope to place in the boys' mess a plate with his name on and the date and the words 'Faithful unto death.' I hope some day you may be able to come and see it there. I have not failed to bring his name prominently before my Admiral."

And when, afterwards, Admiral Jellicoe wrote his official report of the Battle of Jutland, he added these words:

"A report from the Commanding Officer of 'Chester' gives a splendid instance of devotion to duty.

JACK CORNWELL

Boy (1st Class) John Travers Cornwell, of 'Chester,' was mortally wounded early in the action. He nevertheless remained standing alone at a most exposed post, quietly awaiting orders till the end of the action, with the gun's crew dead and wounded all round him. His age was under $16\frac{1}{2}$ years. I regret that he has since died, but I recommend his case for special recognition in justice to his memory, and as an acknowledgment of the high example set by him."

Wonderful, thrilling words these, but so that you may never forget that, as I have said, Jack Cornwell, hero, was a boy like other boys, I am going to copy the last letter

JACK CORNWELL

his father received from him, not many days before the battle. You'll like to read it because it's such an ordinary boyish letter :

" Dear Dad,

"Just a few lines in answer to your most welcome letter, which we received on Monday—first post for a week. That is why you have not had a letter for a long while. Thanks for the stamps you sent me. We are up in the —— somewhere, and they have just put me as sightsetter at a gun. Dear Dad, I have just had to start in pencil, as I have run short of ink, but still, I suppose you don't mind so long as you get a letter, and I am sorry to tell you that poor old A. L. is dead, and I dare say by the time you get this letter she will be buried. I have

JACK CORNWELL

got a lot of letters to send home and about, so I can't afford much more, and we are just about to close up at the gun, so this is all for now : have more next time.

"I remain, your ever-loving son,
"Jack.

P.S.—"Cheer up, Buller me lad, we're not dead yet!"

THE UNKNOWN HERO

Photo. Topical Press.

THE FUNERAL OF JACK CORNWELL.

CHAPTER V

THE UNKNOWN HERO

JOHN TRAVERS CORNWELL, V.C., was buried with all the honours that the Navy and the Country could pay him. The Union Jack covered his coffin, upon which were graven the words "Faithful unto Death," famous sailors stood beside it, the great men of the land followed it to the grave, a Bishop read the burial service. The whole British Empire was represented at the funeral of a hero. And later, the King himself gave to Jack Cornwell's mother the Victoria Cross—the highest award "for valour" that only the noblest heroes wear.

Jack Cornwell died, knowing nothing, thinking nothing of what the great world would think or say of him. He had "carried on all right," that was all he cared about. And, after all, he had done so little—he wished so much he could have done more. His gun had never fired, no orders had come through to him. *"He felt he might be needed—and indeed he might have been."* If only his gun could have hit the Germans. *"His gun would not bear on the enemy."* But he had done all he could.

JACK CORNWELL

He did not even know that his Captain had seen him as he had stood alone by his gun awaiting orders. But he had done his job. He had learned the greatest lesson life could teach him. He had done his duty when, as he thought, no one on earth could see him— with "just his own brave heart and God's help to support him." And that's the greatest lesson life can teach you or me.

This little book is dedicated to the "glorious memory of unknown heroes." I'll tell you why. As I have written it I have thought so often of what might have happened if, instead of steaming

JACK CORNWELL

back to the Grand Fleet, the "Chester" had gone down "with all hands." Ships have been sunk in battle again and again with not a single soul saved to tell the tale—not one. Were there boys and men on such ships as these whose heroism was as great as Jack Cornwell's? Very likely. Are there men and boys, women and girls, all over the world, in a thousand different ways, every day, showing the same pluck and courage and devotion? Yes, I think so. No one hears of them. They are unknown heroes—but heroes just the same.

If no one had lived to tell of the way John Travers Cornwell, V.C., Boy 1st Class, stood alone by his gun in the Battle of Jutland, he, too, would have died an unknown hero. *But a glorious hero just exactly the same.*

THE END